THE STORY OF FRIDA KAHLO

A Biography Book for New Readers

Written by
Susan B. Katz

Illustrated by
Ana Sanfelippo

ROCKRIDGE PRESS

This book is dedicated to artists like my mom, Janice Katz, and my nephew Jacob Katz. May color continue to "bring the happy out of you," as Jacob says, like it did for Frida.

For general information on our other products and services or to obtain technical support, please contact our Customer Care Department within the United States at (866) 744-2665, or outside the United States at (510) 253-0500.

Rockridge Press publishes its books in a variety of electronic and print formats. Some content that appears in print may not be available in electronic books, and vice versa.

Series Designer: Angela Navarra

Interior and Cover Designer: Angela Navarra

Art Producer: Hillary Frileck

Editor: Orli Zuravicky

Production Editor: Jenna Dutton

Illustration © 2019 Ana Sanfelippo; Creative Market/Mia Buono, pp 3, 11, 22, 32, 35, 45, 54; Author Photo courtesy of ©Jeanne Marquis; Illustrator Photo courtesy of ©Miriam Herrera

ISBN: Print 978-1-64611-160-2 | eBook 978-1-64611-161-9

R1

Printed in China

CONTENTS

CHAPTER 1

AN ARTIST IS BORN

Meet Frida Kahlo

Frida Kahlo was no ordinary child. She was very sick and spent much of her time at home in bed. Frida's sisters went off to school, so she was often alone. That's when her imagination would come alive! Frida invented an imaginary friend. She pictured the two of them climbing out of a pretend hole in the window and into a fantasy world, where they would dance and play together. Then, Frida began drawing her imaginary stories. Soon, an artist was born!

As Frida got older, she faced lots of challenges. Many things in her life changed. One thing that stayed the same was her incredible imagination. It helped her become one of the most famous Mexican artists of all time.

Frida spent much of her life sick and in pain. Painting was Frida's way of showing how she was feeling and sharing her thoughts with the

JUMP IN THE THINK TANK

How do you think art helped Frida express herself? How does art make a difference in the world?

world. Frida loved her country. She used many **symbols** of Mexican culture in her paintings. Frida liked to wear fancy flowers and flowing dresses. She had many pets: dogs, deer, and even spider monkeys! Frida loved animals, so they fill many of her paintings.

Frida was strong and independent. She was born in the early 1900s. At that time, few women were thought of as true artists. But that didn't stop Frida. Women also did not usually work outside of the home, go to high school, or travel. Frida did all of these things during her life—and more!

> "Painting completed my life."

Frida's Mexico

Frida Kahlo was born in Mexico on July 6, 1907. She was given a very long name: Magdalena Carmen Frida Kahlo y Calderón. Her family called her Frida. Frida loved her country for its beautiful people, delicious food, colorful festivals, and tall mountains.

As she got older, Frida saw that there were some problems with Mexico's **government**. The leader of Mexico was not listening to what

the people wanted. The **Mexican Revolution** was beginning. People marched in the streets. Sometimes Frida and her mother welcomed soldiers into their home, the Blue House, for a hot meal and a break from the war. Frida listened to the soldiers talk about how unfair life was for workers. She decided she wanted to help build a fair society for all.

Frida's father, Guillermo Kahlo, was a Jewish Hungarian-German **immigrant**. Her mother, Matilde Calderón y González, was a ***mestiza***

Mexican woman. Matilde's family was both Mexican Native American and Spanish. Frida was much closer to her father. He was a photographer and painter. He also shared her love of art and animals. Guillermo was very kind to Frida when she was sick and loved her very much. Frida always felt like she was his favorite child. Frida's father let her use his paint and brushes. Her parents even had a special easel made for her so that she could paint while lying down in bed!

Frida's path to fame was long and surprising. Along the way she met and married a famous artist. Later, she had art **exhibitions** of her own! Let's find out how Frida healed from sickness and rose to the top.

WHEN?

1872 Frida's dad, Guillermo, is born.

1876 Frida's mom, Matilde, is born.

1891 Frida's dad moves to Mexico.

1904 Guillermo builds the Blue House.

1907 Frida is born.

1910 The Mexican Revolution begins.

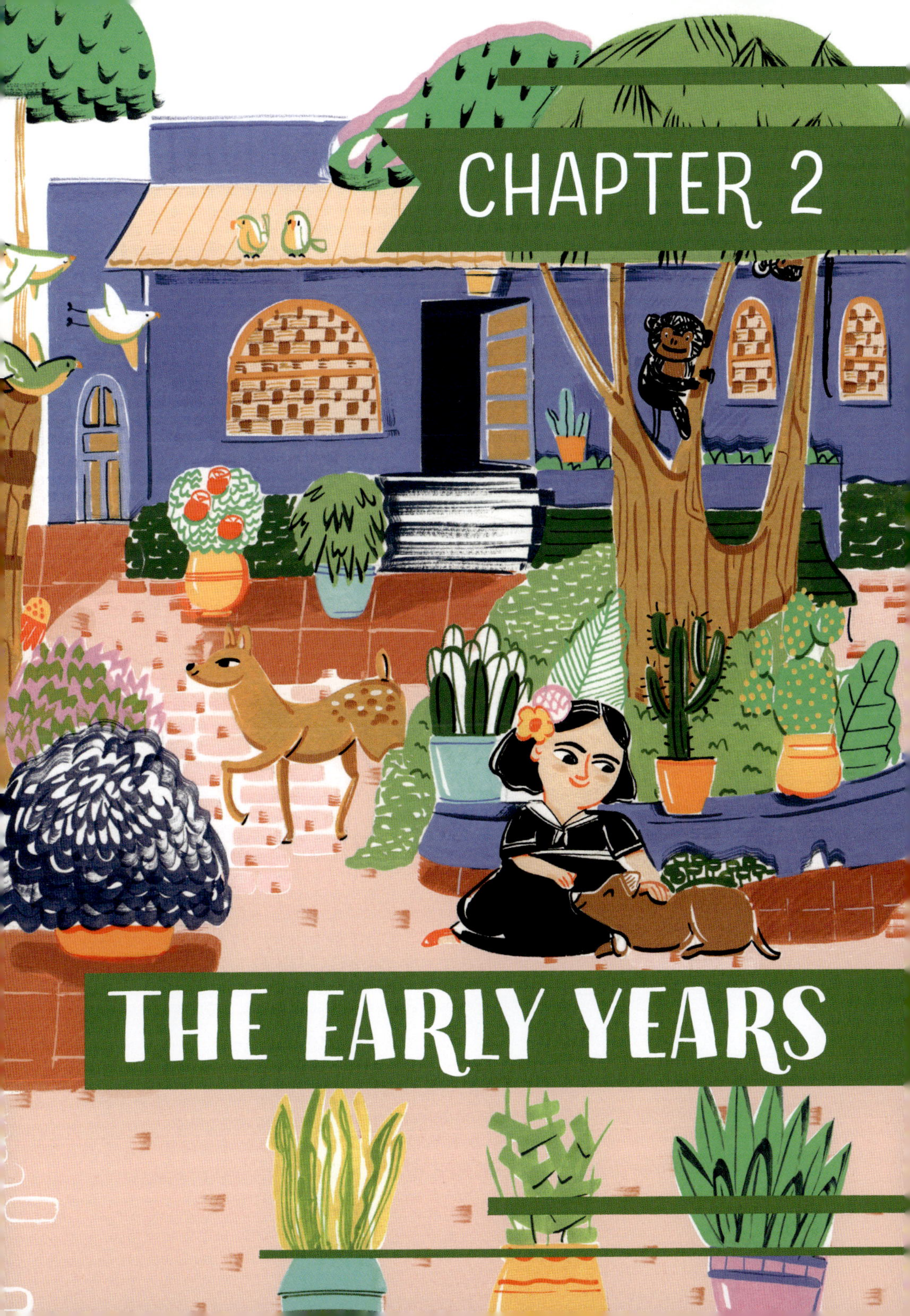

CHAPTER 2

THE EARLY YEARS

Growing up in Coyoacán, Mexico

Frida was born in *La Casa Azul,* or the Blue House. Frida's house was very special to her because her father built and painted it. The house was in Coyoacán, Mexico, a village just outside of Mexico City. Frida lived most of her life there.

When Frida was six years old, she got a disease called **polio**. Frida had high fevers and was tired all the time. She had to stay in bed for months. Polio made Frida's right leg hurt, and caused it to be shorter and thinner than her left leg. She was bullied by other kids. They called her Frida *Pata de Palo,* or Peg Leg Frida. Frida was sad that she had to stay home in bed, but she was happy that she could spend so much time with her dad.

When she got better, Frida and her father went on trips together. The Mexican government

wanted Guillermo to take photographs all over Mexico. On their trips, Frida's father taught her how to draw people and nature. Frida's imagination went wild! After each trip, Frida ran back to her room to draw all the beauty she had seen before she forgot it. She included

JUMP IN THE THINK TANK

What is it about animals that makes people feel better?

symbols like doves and a Mexican flag made out of *papel picado,* or cut paper, in her drawings.

Frida's love of nature meant that she brought all kinds of bugs and animals into the Blue House. Her mother didn't like this at all, but her father encouraged her curiosity. After looking through a **microscope**,

Kahlo Family Tree

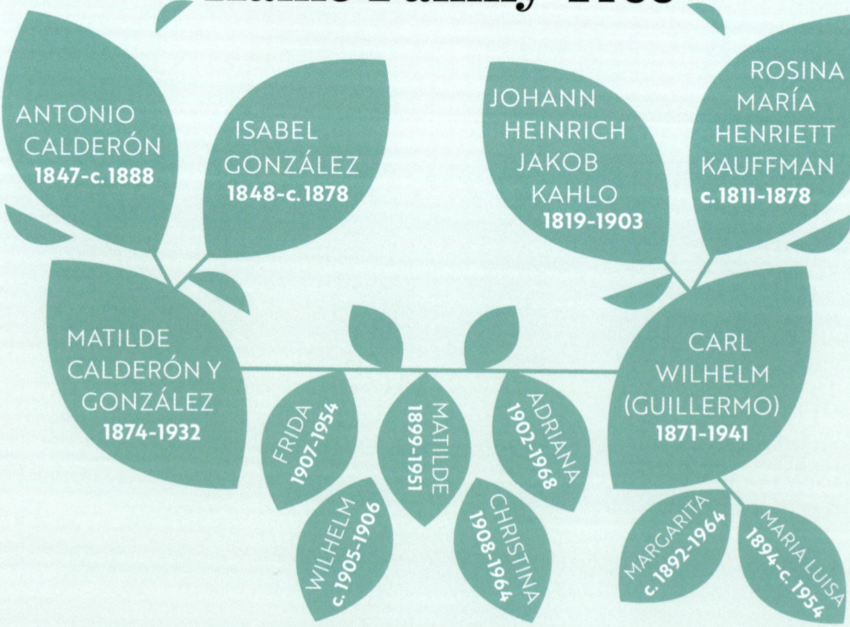

sometimes Frida painted what she saw up close. Big bugs looked really cool on her canvas!

Dreams of Becoming a Doctor

Frida was a very smart student. She was so smart that she was accepted into the best high school in Mexico City. Not many girls were invited to the National Preparatory School. Frida was one of only 35 girls in a school with more than 2,000 boys! Frida wanted to become a doctor, but she often misbehaved in class. She liked to play tricks on people and was once even kicked out of school!

During her high school years, the Mexican Revolution continued to grow. When Frida was old enough, she joined the people's fight with some of her friends and her boyfriend, Alejandro Gómez Arias. Her friends were also interested in reading and talking about important books.

MYTH	&	FACT
Frida's art was only famous in Mexico.		Even during Frida's lifetime, her art was shown in Paris, New York, and San Francisco. She soon became world famous.

Many artists were invited to come to the school to create giant paintings on the walls, called murals. The murals showed what was happening in Mexico during that time. Most artists were men. In 1922, when Frida was 15, a famous Mexican artist named Diego Rivera came to her school to paint a mural. Frida even

played tricks on *him*! She had a crush on Diego. Putting soap on the stairs he'd climb was her strange way of showing it!

WHEN?

Frida falls ill with polio.	Frida begins at the National Preparatory School.	Frida meets Diego Rivera at school.
1913	**1922**	**1922**

CHAPTER 3

A LIFE SAVED

Changing Course

Frida went to and from school in an old wooden bus. On September 17, 1925, when Frida was 18 years old, she and Alejandro were on the bus when it got into an accident. Frida was seriously hurt and almost died. The accident put her back in bed for months. Frida had 32 surgeries and was in a full body cast! The doctors didn't think she would ever walk again—if she survived at all.

Being in bed for months on end frustrated Frida. All she had was her imagination and art. Luckily, those were as strong as ever. She started drawing colorful butterflies on her cast. She also painted pictures of her feet. They were all she could see! Later, her parents gave her a special easel and put a mirror over her head. She started painting **self-portraits**, or paintings of herself. Frida said that she painted herself because she was alone so much that she knew herself better than anyone or anything else. Her first real painting was called *Self-Portrait in a Velvet Dress*.

Frida used art to express her sadness and pain. When she was sad, the colors and objects in her paintings were dark, dreary, and sometimes spooky. When she was happy, Frida's paintings were bright and cheery. Frida often felt broken inside, and she showed that through her art. Eventually, Frida surprised her family and doctors by learning to walk again!

> "I am **not sick**. I am broken. But I am **happy to be alive** as long as I can **paint**."

The accident left Frida with many broken bones that changed how her body looked. She was often in pain and she walked with a limp. Frida began to wear long dresses to cover up her body. She also wore high-necked blouses to cover up the brace she had to wear. Frida dressed this way to cover her injuries, but her unique style of "Frida fashion" became famous along with her art.

Meeting Diego, Again

Frida was still very interested in the Mexican Revolution. She found a new group of friends who liked to talk about **politics**, art, and books. She went to a lot of parties with them. She wore a star on her jacket as a symbol of the revolution.

At one party, Frida was reintroduced to Diego Rivera. A few days later, Frida asked him to look at her paintings and give his honest opinion. Diego really liked her work and began to teach her more about painting. Diego was about

JUMP IN THE THINK TANK

Sometimes when bad things happen, good things can come out of them. Can you think of times, either in your life or during history, when this happened?

20 years older than Frida. Still, after spending time together they fell in love. On August 21, 1929, Frida and Diego got married. Frida's parents did not approve of their marriage. They

said that it was like an elephant marrying a dove.

After the terrible accident, Frida was headed for exciting adventures as an artist and the wife of a famous muralist. Little did she know what her new life would offer. She would get the chance to travel to different countries, meet lots of interesting people, and even show off her own art!

WHEN?

Frida gets in an accident. She starts to paint.	Frida re-meets Diego at a party.	Frida and Diego get married.
1925	**1928**	**1929**

CHAPTER 4
WORLD TRAVELERS

Traveling with Diego

After Frida and Diego got married, Frida spent most of her time learning to cook her husband's favorite foods and helping him prepare for long days of painting. Soon, she stopped working on her own paintings. At that time in history, wives were expected to put their husbands' needs first.

In 1930, Diego was asked to paint some murals in San Francisco, California. Frida joined him. Once there, the couple were invited to many fancy parties at night. During the day, Frida was alone a lot while Diego was painting. She did not feel at home in the United States. Frida missed Mexico and her family terribly. Diego, on the other hand, was enjoying his fame in San Francisco. He and Frida often fought about whether to stay in the United States or go back to Mexico.

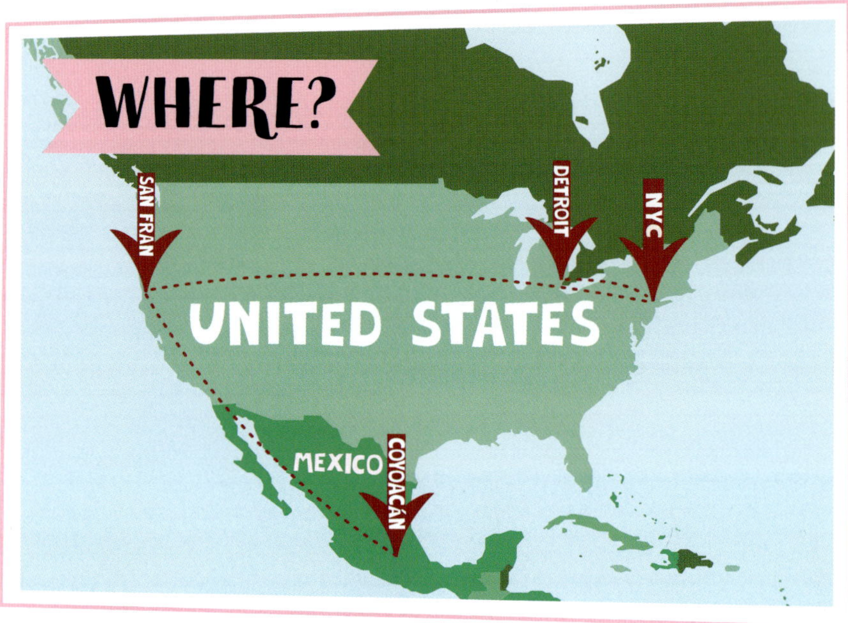

It had been years since her bus accident, but Frida still had a lot of pain in her leg. While in San Francisco, she met a doctor named Leo Eloesser. They became fast friends. Dr. Eloesser treated Frida for her pain. Then she finally started to paint again. She painted *Frieda and Diego Rivera,* a portrait of them on their wedding day. The painting shows Diego holding his painter's palette and brushes. He is much bigger than Frida. The painting seems to express her

loneliness. The San Francisco Society of Women Artists loved it and included the painting in their sixth annual exhibition. It was Frida's first painting to be shown in public!

A Bridge Between Homes

In early 1931, Frida and Diego moved back to Mexico. The couple fought a lot. Diego decided to

JUMP IN THE THINK TANK

How do you show your sadness or frustration? Do you draw, write, or do something else to let it out?

have two houses built and connected by a bridge in San Ángel, in Mexico City. They each had a private space but could still visit each other easily. The outside of Frida's house was painted blue, just like *La Casa Azul*.

In November, the Museum of Modern Art in New York City decided to host an exhibit of Diego's art. The Riveras sailed on a boat from Mexico to New York.

MYTH & FACT

MYTH: Frida became famous because of Diego Rivera.

FACT: Frida's talent and connections with other artists made her famous.

Frida felt very homesick in New York, so she painted *My Dress Hangs There*. The painting shows a clothesline stretching across New

York City. Frida's traditional Mexican dress is hanging on it. The painting also shows garbage cans, toilets, and buildings on fire. Frida didn't seem to like New York City. Her body and clothes were in the United States, but her heart and soul were in Mexico.

In 1932, Diego was invited to paint a mural at the Detroit Institute of Arts in Michigan. The Riveras packed their suitcases again and moved

to Detroit. Frida was tired of the United States. She really wanted to go back to Mexico and she wasn't shy about telling Diego how she felt.

When the Riveras finally moved home to Mexico and settled into their homes, Frida started painting a lot more. People began to see that Diego wasn't the only one who painted well—Frida did, too! The University of Mexico invited Frida to put her paintings in a group exhibit. There, someone from a gallery in New York saw Frida's paintings. He asked Frida if he could include some of her paintings in an exhibit in New York. Frida started painting right away!

WHEN?

Frida and Diego go to San Francisco, California.

1930

Frida's first exhibit. They move back to Mexico, then to New York.

1931

Frida and Diego move to Michigan, then return to Mexico.

1932

CHAPTER 5

FRIDA'S TIME TO SHINE

Frida in New York

In 1938, Frida's art was part of an exhibit in New York City. She was finally being seen outside of Mexico as an artist herself, and not just the wife of an artist. This trip was about Frida's art. It was one of the first times *any* Mexican artist—male or female—had been offered an exhibit outside of Mexico! Since Frida was a woman, this made the invitation even more amazing!

Frida's work was different from anything people had ever seen. Her art stood out. So did Frida. She did not care if her art **offended** people. She was strong and confident. She did not change her views, her art, or her traditional

Mexican clothes to fit in with New Yorkers. Half of Frida's paintings sold at the New York show!

Some people wondered if Frida was a **surrealist**. A surrealist is an artist who paints real things in ways that make them look unreal, like they come from a dream or a nightmare. Later, others called Frida's art **magical realism** because she painted real things with a magical touch. For example, in *The Wounded Deer*, she painted a realistic deer that had her own human head on it! Still others called Frida's masterpieces symbolic because they seemed to tell hidden stories.

> "They thought I was a Surrealist, but I wasn't. I never painted dreams or nightmares. I painted my own reality."

Frida said that she just painted what she felt her world was really like. She felt like she had two lives and two hearts. She tried to show this in *The Two Fridas,* where she painted what look like twin Fridas, holding hands, their hearts connected by a long vein.

After Frida's success in New York, the Louvre Museum in Paris, France, bought one of Frida's self-portraits. For that piece, Frida used different materials like aluminum together with colorful paints. This self-portrait, called *The Frame,* became a part of the Louvre's permanent collection in 1939. Frida was the first 20th-century Mexican artist to have a painting in their galleries!

Off to Paris!

When it was time for Frida to go to Paris for an exhibit at a gallery, she went by herself. Diego stayed in Mexico. She was feeling more confident than ever because so many people liked her work. Frida was outgoing and made many friends all over the world. She became good friends with an American artist named **Georgia O'Keeffe**. The two wrote letters to each other and visited sometimes.

In Paris, several famous artists like **Joan Miró** and **Pablo Picasso** came to her exhibit and congratulated her. **Curators** and museum visitors loved Frida's

JUMP IN THE THINK TANK

How do you think a group of artists, like Frida's friends, help support one another? Do you have a group that supports you in something?

colorful style of dress, unique artwork, big, bushy eyebrows, and can-do attitude. Frida had a difficult past, but she made lemonade out of lemons: She created art out of pain and loneliness.

Frida became part of a growing group of artists in Paris, who were mostly men. While Diego supported Frida's art, he missed her and wanted her to come home. Still, even after she returned, Frida and Diego continued to fight quite often.

Frida was having a lot of success in the art world, but her marriage was failing. She still

had pain in her bad leg and in her spine. Now she was using a cane to walk. Strong and determined, Frida kept on going. She knew she could face whatever life brought her way.

Frida has her first solo show in New York City.

1938

Frida has a show in Paris.

1939

WHEN?

CHAPTER 6

FAME FINDS FRIDA

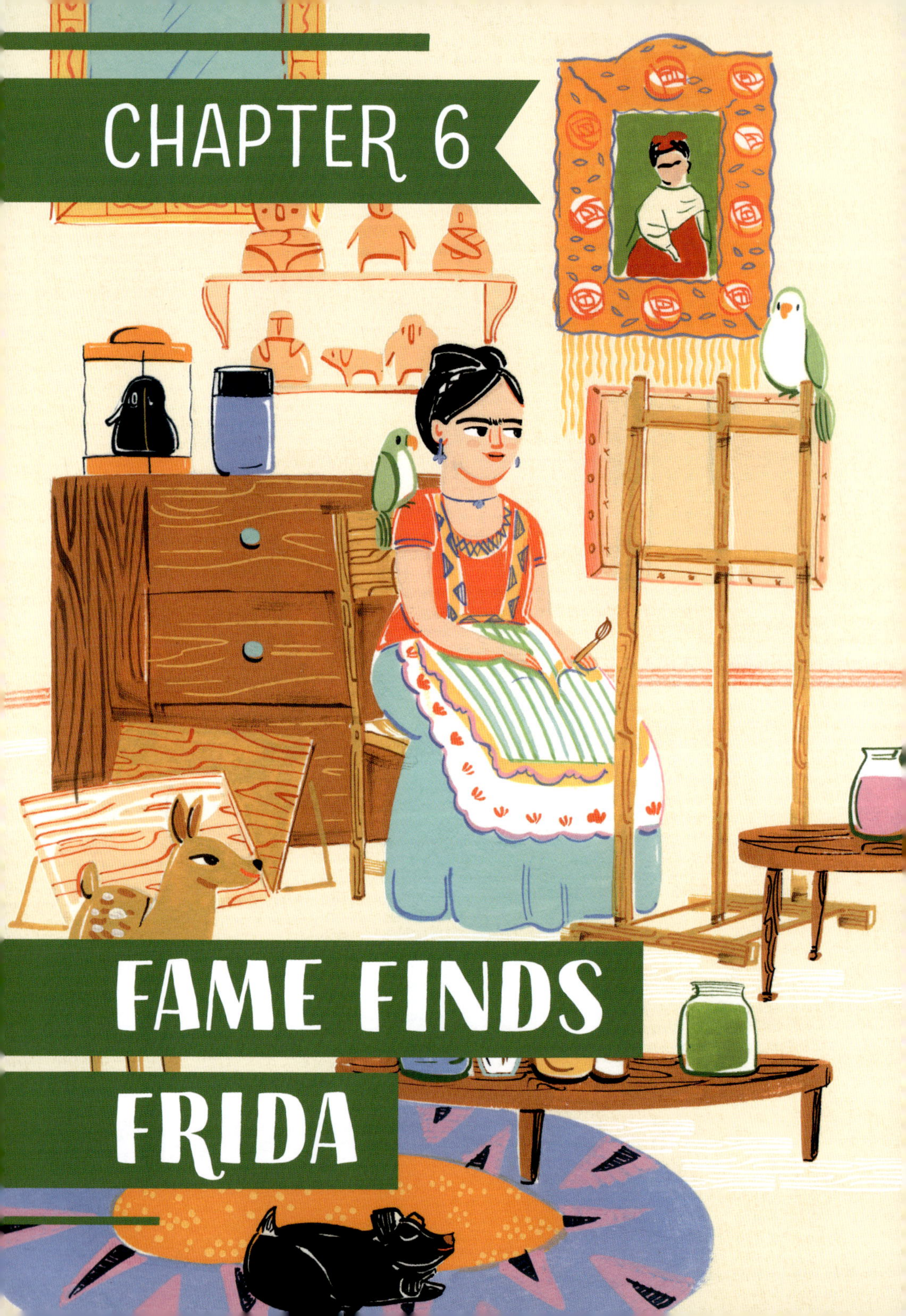

Ups and Downs

Frida returned to Mexico in 1939, but she was still feeling homesick. She and Diego decided to move back into her childhood home—the Blue House. They had many animals, such as spider monkeys, a fawn, and several dogs. Since she painted the things around her, Frida included many of her animals in her artwork. She *and* her pets were becoming famous!

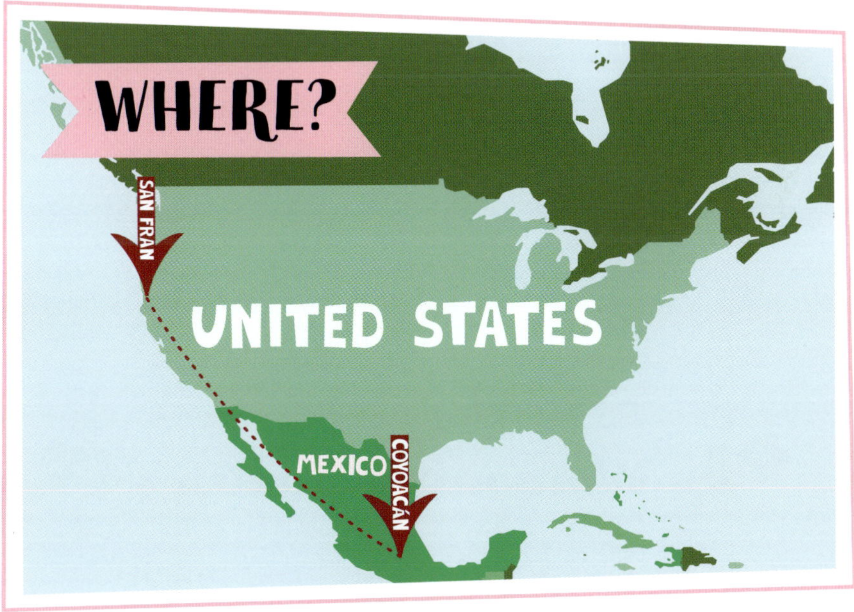

While her career as an artist was doing great, her marriage was not. After many years of struggling and arguing, Frida and Diego decided to get divorced. Diego moved out of the Blue House and back into one of their houses in San Ángel. Heartbroken, Frida painted her pain into a work of art called *The Wounded Table*. It shows a bleeding table with human legs. Some say it is a symbol of Frida's feelings about her marriage being broken by divorce.

> "Feet, what do I need them for when I have wings to fly?"

Frida's health was also getting worse. The pain in her spine and legs made it hard for her to walk.

Frida's Worsening Health

Just a year later, Frida's health was much worse. Doctors in Mexico wanted to operate on her spine. Frida wanted Dr. Eloesser's opinion before she agreed to anything. She went to visit him in San Francisco, where Diego happened to be painting another mural. Even though they were divorced, Frida and Diego kept in touch. They still loved each other deeply.

JUMP IN THE THINK TANK

The Blue House was a place where Frida felt safe and happy. Do you have a place like that in your life?

Dr. Eloesser told Frida that she didn't need surgery, but she *did* need to stay in bed. He also convinced her to remarry Diego. On Diego's 54th birthday, December 8, 1940, the couple got married for a second time. Frida was happy to be married to Diego again. She and Diego returned to the Blue House. There, Frida could rest and heal.

Even though Frida was stuck in bed at home, her paintings continued to travel the world. In 1940, her art was included in an exhibit at the Institute of Contemporary Art in Boston, Massachusetts. Frida's *Self-Portrait with Braid* made it into a show at the Museum of Modern Art in New York City called *Twentieth Century Portraits*.

While Frida was recovering, her father passed away suddenly in 1941. The two of them were so close that his death put Frida into a deep depression, or sadness. The only things that made her feel better were *La Casa Azul*, all of her animals, and, after a while, her art.

Life went on without her beloved dad, and Frida kept painting. She knew he would have wanted her to. Galleries and museums all over the world were asking to display her work. She started teaching art, which filled her soul with a different kind of happiness. Frida had Diego and many teachers in the art world. Now she got to be one for other young artists!

WHEN?

1939: Frida has a show in Paris. The Riveras move home and divorce.

1940: Frida goes to San Francisco. She and Diego remarry.

1941: Frida's father dies.

CHAPTER 7

A FIGHTER TILL THE END

The Student Becomes the Teacher

When Frida began her career as an artist, Diego was like a teacher to her and she was like his student. Years later, Frida became a teacher at the National School of Painting, Sculpture, and Engraving in Mexico City (known in Spanish as *La Esmeralda*). Frida's students loved her and admired her work very much. They called themselves *"Los Fridos,"* or "Frida's Fans." Unfortunately, after Frida spent just a few months teaching, her health got worse. But Frida was determined to keep teaching. She invited her students to the Blue House so they could learn from her there while she was resting and healing.

She also kept painting and exhibiting her art in Mexico. Two important paintings during this time were *Roots,* a painting showing Frida's connection to Mexico, and *Self-Portrait with*

JUMP IN THE THINK TANK

Why is it important for people who were once students to become teachers?

Monkeys. Frida never lost her love of animals, and this painting showed that!

The Final Exhibition

Frida always wanted to have a solo show of her work in Mexico, her beloved home. Finally, in 1953, an exhibition of her work was planned at a modern art gallery in Mexico City. Frida was so sick that the doctor told her she had to stay in bed. Ever clever, Frida had men lift her on a stretcher and carry her into the gallery, making a grand entrance. There, they placed her in her canopy bed, which had been brought in before. That way, she stayed in bed while still attending her opening party. She told her doctor that she did follow his orders and stay in bed—she had just brought the bed to her exhibit!

Frida's body got weaker and she could no longer take the pain. Sadly, she died in the Blue House on July 13, 1954. It was just a few days after she turned 47. Since Frida was such a strong, talented, and amazing role model, her body was placed at the Palace of Fine Arts in Mexico City for the public to view. Frida was so important as a Mexican artist that everyone wanted to honor her and have a chance to say goodbye.

Frida's artwork changed our world. Her fame brought attention to Mexico and helped women artists around the world gain more respect. One of the last paintings that Frida created was called *Viva la Vida*, or "Long Live Life." Though Frida is gone, her memory and art live on in museums and art schools around the globe today.

> "I paint **flowers** so they will **not die**."

Frida could have kept her art to herself and been known only as the wife of a famous muralist. She could have let bad luck and poor health get her down. Instead, she did the opposite. Frida used her pain and sadness to paint beautiful self-portraits and tell stories through her art. Then, she shared it with the world. Her work showed Mexico's beauty to people around the world. It helped people get to know Frida and see her struggles.

Through her art, Frida wasn't shy about commenting on things like the pollution in New York or the Mexican Revolution. Today, Frida Kahlo is not only known for her artwork or her bushy unibrow—she is known for her courage and ability to keep going through tough times. Since her death, Frida's artwork has gained even more attention. Her masterpieces are on display in museums in San Francisco, Boston, New York, Paris and, of course, Mexico City. *¡Viva Frida!*

WHEN?

1946 — Frida starts teaching at *La Esmeralda.*

1953 — Frida has her last show in Mexico City.

1954 — Frida dies in *La Casa Azul.*

CHAPTER 8

SO . . . WHO WAS FRIDA KAHLO?

Challenge Accepted!

Now that you know so much about Frida's life and work, let's test your new knowledge in a little who, what, when, where, why, and how quiz. Feel free to look back in the text to find the answers if you need to, but try to remember first.

1 Where was Frida born?

→ A San Francisco, California

→ B Detroit, Michigan

→ C Coyoacán, Mexico

→ D New York City, New York

2 What disease did Frida get when she was just six years old?

→ A Measles

→ B Polio

→ C Mumps

→ D Chicken pox

3 Why did Frida paint lying down?

→ A She was sick and injured so she had to stay in bed.

→ B She didn't like standing.

→ C She was lazy.

→ D Her parents made her.

4 Who was Frida's husband?

→ A Pablo Picasso

→ B Joan Miró

→ C Auguste Rodin

→ D Diego Rivera

5 How old was Frida when she first met her husband at her school?

→ A 12

→ B 18

→ C 15

→ D 21

6 What did Frida like to paint?

→ A Animals and self-portraits

→ B Maps and mountains

→ C Ice cream and igloos

→ D The moon and sun

7 When and where did Frida have her first solo exhibit in Mexico?

→ A 1907 in the Blue House

→ B 1953 at the Gallery of Contemporary Art in Mexico City

→ C 1930 in the houses with a bridge between them

→ D 1922 at her high school

8 Why is Frida considered a female role model?

→ A She was one of the first Mexican female artists to be recognized.

→ B She walked with a cane.

→ C She was a famous opera singer.

→ D She married a well-known artist.

9 What three cities held exhibits of Frida's art?

→ A San Francisco, California; Philadelphia, Pennsylvania; and Rome, Italy

→ B Detroit, Michigan; Taos, New Mexico; and San José, Costa Rica

→ C Paris, France; Mexico City, Mexico; and New York City, New York

→ D Miami, Florida; Mexico City, Mexico; and Maui, Hawaii

10 Who was Frida very close to?

→ A Her daughter

→ B Her mom

→ C Her cousin

→ D Her dad

Answers: 1. C; 2. B; 3. A; 4. D; 5. C; 6. A; 7. B; 8. A; 9. C; 10. D

Our World

Frida's life and work changed our world today. Let's look at a few things that are different because of the way Frida lived and created art.

→ Female artists are far more famous now than they were before Frida's time. They also earn more money for their paintings. In 1977, Frida's estate sold her first painting for just $19,000. In 2016, one of Frida's paintings sold for $8 million! Shortly before Frida was born, women were often not allowed to exhibit their work in museums. Today, female artists now make up 46 percent of all recognized artists.

→ Mexican culture and symbols are becoming more a part of American culture. We see *papel picado* (cut paper) doves and other Mexican symbols in many schools, restaurants, and museums. This is partly because people have emigrated from Mexico to the United States. Frida's use of these symbols also helped the world understand what they mean and embrace them.

→ Sometimes wives stand behind their husbands, sort of in their shadows. Frida stood out from Diego and made a name for herself. Her example has helped women focus on their own careers and talents. Frida's personality and desire to tell her story through art has inspired many other women (and men) to do the same in their own ways.

JUMP IN THE THINK TANK FOR MORE!

Now let's think a little more about what Frida did and how her art and courage affected the world we currently live in.

→ How has Frida's art, and the attention she got for it, helped other artists be seen and shine?

→ How does Frida's determination through her illness and injuries inspire you to push through tough times?

→ How did painting self-portraits allow Frida to tell the story of her life? How could you tell your story? In writing? Through music or art?

Glossary

curators: People who gather and take care of art in a museum, zoo, or other place

exhibitions: Displays of works of art in art galleries or museums

Georgia O'Keeffe: An American artist best known for painting large flowers, bones (or skulls), New York skyscrapers, and New Mexico landscapes

government: The rules, system, and people that organize a country, state, city, or local community

Joan Miró: A Spanish painter, sculptor, and ceramicist born in Barcelona

immigrant: A person who moves to a new country and settles there

magical realism: Painting imaginary or fantasy scenes in a realistic style

mestiza/mestizo: The Spanish word for someone who has mixed European and Native American blood

Mexican Revolution: A civil war in Mexico that began when people tried to overthrow the dictator, Porfirio Díaz, in 1910. It ended when a new political party took control in the 1930s.

microscope: A tool that magnifies small objects that are too hard to see and makes them look larger

offended: When someone is upset by something someone else says or does

Pablo Picasso: A famous Spanish painter who used collage and mixed-media. He painted many blue paintings and many with cubes and 3-D faces.

polio: A virus that can cause weak muscles, muscle pain, and sometimes death

politics: The way groups of people (like countries, cities, schools, or companies) make decisions about rules and laws

self-portraits: A painting, sculpture, or photograph that an artist creates of themself

Surrealists: A group of artists in the 20th century who painted real things in ways that made them look unreal, like they came from a dream or a nightmare

symbols/symbolism: An object taking the place of an idea or another object. Symbols usually stand for or mean something.

Bibliography

Brooks, Mike. "Chronology." *Frida Kahlo Fans*. Accessed September 25, 2019. http://www.fridakahlofans.com/chronologyenglish.html.

Frida Kahlo Foundation. "Biography." http://www.frida-kahlo-foundation.org/biography.html.

Grimberg, Salomon. *Frida Kahlo: Song of Herself*. London: Merrell, 2008.

Herrera, Hayden. *Frida: A Biography of Frida Kahlo*. New York: Harper Perennial, 2002.

Kahlo, Frida. *Diary of Frida Kahlo: An Intimate Self-Portrait*. New York: Abrams, 2005.

Schulmann, Didier. "Frida Kahlo in Paris." Accessed October 5, 2019. https://artsandculture.google.com/theme/8gIi85WrSrdVLw.

Sills, Leslie. *Inspirations: Stories About Women Artists: Georgia O'Keeffe, Frida Kahlo, Alice Neel, and Faith Ringgold*. New York: Albert Whitman and Company, 1989.

Wikiquote. "Quotes of Frida Kahlo: 1925–1945." Accessed September 22, 2019. https://en.wikiquote.org/wiki/Frida_Kahlo.

Acknowledgments

First and foremost, I want to honor the memory of Frida Kahlo for being such a talented and sassy soul, ever independent and creative. It was an inspiration and an honor to research and write about her as we share Hungarian-Jewish heritage, a love of art, and have lived in many of the same places—Detroit, San Francisco, and Latin America. I appreciate my outstanding editor, Orli, who entrusted me with this book and guided me with grace, precision, and determination. I want to thank my parents, Janice and Ray, for their encouragement. To my brother, Steve, thanks! Kudos to my talented writers' group—Andrew, Brandi, Evan, Kyle, and Sonia. In memory of my grandma Grace, my aunt Judy, Joe McClain, and my mentor, Ilse. To my nephews, Sam, Jacob, and David, and my niece, Sofia. Thanks to the entire Callisto team! I am supported by family and friends: Michelle G., Susan, Ann and Greg, Danielle, Jeanne, Deborah, Laurie, Tanya, Carla, Julia and Ira, Maureen, Amparo, Michael, Ricardo, Alejandra, Arden, Jen, Tami, Karen, Annie, Crystal, Bryan, Jessica, Marji, Marcy, Lara, Anita and Bob, Jerry, Nena and Mel, Jami, Stacy and Rick, Michelle R., Chalmers, Violeta, Diana y Juanca, and Sylvia Boorstein.

—SBK

About the Author

SUSAN B. KATZ is an award-winning bilingual author, National Board Certified teacher, educational consultant, and keynote speaker. She taught for more than 25 years. Susan has published five books with Scholastic, Random House, and Barefoot Books. *Meditation Station,* a book about trains and mindfulness, is due out in fall 2020 with Bala Kids (Shambhala). Her other titles include *ABC, Baby Me!*, *My Mama Earth* (Moonbeam Gold Award winner for best picture book and named a "top green toy" by Education.com), *ABC School's for Me* (illustrated by Lynn Munsinger), and *All Year Round,* which she translated into Spanish as *Un Año Redondo* for Scholastic. Susan is also the executive director of ConnectingAuthors.org, a national nonprofit bringing children's book authors and illustrators into schools. She served as the strategic partner manager for authors at Facebook. When she's not writing, Susan enjoys traveling, salsa dancing, and spending time at the beach. You can find out more about her books and school visits at **SusanKatzBooks.com.**

About the Illustrator

ANA SANFELIPPO is from Buenos Aires, Argentina. Her work includes illustrations for books, magazines, patterns and products. She has published many children's books and has shown her work at exhibitions in Argentina, Slovakia, England, Canada and Spain. She combines many by hand techniques, and loves creating natural sceneries and funny characters with many vibrant colors.